TENNIS

Written By:
Herbert I. Kavet

Illustrated By:
Martin Riskin

Ivory Tower Publishing Co., Inc.
125 Walnut Street
P.O. Box 9132
Watertown, MA 02272-9132
Telephone #: (617) 923-1111   Fax #: (617) 923-8839

Introduction

Playing tennis as a youth, I was teaching the game to a friend. Winning the first point I shouted, "15 - Nothing." My friend looked doubtful and questioned how I could get 15 points so quickly. I shut him up and winning the next point announced, "30 - Nothing." Well, he was convinced now of my underhanded methods and stormed off the court wanting nothing more to do with tennis.

Considering the potential for injury, the frustrations, and the ever-increasing expense, it was probably a good choice.

"No, No, the first set was 6-4 and you served and started on the sunny side, then I served and it has to be 4-3."

"Marie is playing the distraction game for all it's worth today."

"I think it's to the left of the poison ivy."

Tennis – A Game of Ethical Dilemmas

Tennis is a gentleman's game. It's a game played with sportsmanship and politeness where the players act as their own umpires. Say a ball is hit so hard you didn't see if it went in or out. Sportsmanship dictates that if you don't know, it's good. On the other hand, simple logic would suggest anything hit that hard probably went out. A good compromise in ethical dilemmas like this, is the "just out" call which mixes justice with a sort of face-saving compliment for your opponent. Remember those words, "JUST OUT".

The "Just Out" Guilty Look

"So you built it yourself."

"Honest, I just opened them yesterday!"

Excuses

All good weekend players know that it's important to establish your excuses before stepping onto the court. Winning the excuse game enables you to concentrate on the tennis itself knowing all the joy has already been taken from a possible win by your opponent.

The classics:
> Knee
> Back
> Tennis Elbow

Complaints should be occasionally supplemented with the more sophisticated ailments: rotation cuff, hip extension, and anteria crucia ligament.

Excuses

Watching two real pros present their excuses before a game is often more entertaining than the tennis itself.

Player A: "Oh, my knee's been bothering me."
Player B: "Yeah, well I have to see the chiropractor for my back this afternoon."
Player A: "That guy's great, told me not to throw the ball too high because of my shoulder."
Player B: "You really have to watch that or it'll develop into tennis elbow like I have."

You get the picture. It's kind of like a medical bidding game decorated by an assortment of braces and pads.

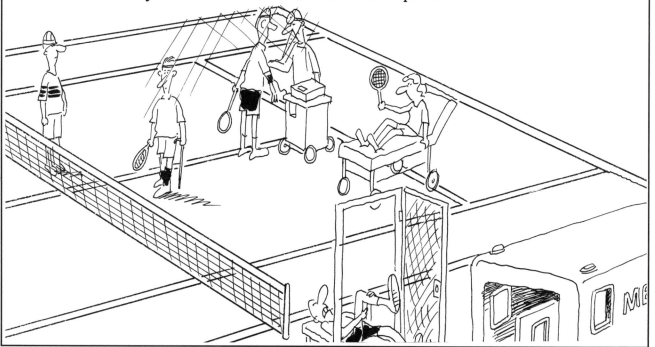

"There has to be some limit to these
oversized racquets."

"That's why you never have husbands and wives as partners."

The Serve

Whey you serve you're trying to get the ball into a teeny box, all but about two inches of which seems to be totally covered by the net. What's more, your opponent knows (unless he or she is very stupid) exactly which side of the court you are going to hit the ball to and is all set and ready waiting to ram it back down your throat.

The Serve

When you receive, however, the court looks normally like this. Worse, your opponent gets two chances to decapitate you.

"Heads up."

Fighting your way up the tennis ladder.

"Just Out"

A few more words on this very important call. It's used to squelch any thought, on the part of your opponent, that there is the smallest possibility of a dishonest bone in your body. You're telling her or him that the shot was basically a good one but that it was out, through no fault of their own, by a tiny inconsequential margin.

"Just Out"

Be careful using this call on clay or hartrue courts where the impression of the ball can be seen unless you smoosch the spot a little with your foot.

"These mosquitoes are getting bigger every year."

"There goes the honeymoon."

Strategy

The most effective strategy for 97% of all players is to hope the ball will hit a crack, pebble or bad spot on the court. This has been proven to be much more effective than the difficult placement of shots which most often leads to the ball going out. The way it's done is, as you follow through, you pray, "Hit a crack, hit a crack, take a bad bounce." To make this strategy more effective, real serious players add to the obstructions on the side of the court they are leaving, and naturally try to smooth or clean up the pebbles and holes the dastardly opponent has left.

"Jonathan just plays to relax."

"It's convenient, but you sure lose a lot of balls."

Wood Shots

Everyone knows that more points are scored off what used to be called wood shots, but now more correctly should be called carbon fiber, Titanium, ceramic boron shots. These cleverly hit but flukey shots are so erratic as to be almost impossible to return. The wood (DBA carbon fiber, titanium, etc.) shot is initiated by taking your eye off the ball as soon as it crosses the net. A good club player learns to rely on these shots rather than treat them as random bits of luck.

"Maybe we'd better let it dry out a little more."

"Winthrop once played on a grass court."

"Whaddaya mean that was a warm up?"

The Backhand

Everyone knows how hard it is to hit the ball on your backhand side and unscrupulous opponents take advantage of this by insisting on hitting the ball there. Short of refusing to play with these scoundrels, the best way to handle a backhand shot is to run around it and hit with your powerful and dependable forehand. Studies show that 84% of the time this is the most effective way to handle a backhand shot. Practice it and your game will improve. No kidding.

"Ok, let's forget about top spin for now."

"Not quite that much follow through."

"Please hit it over one more time. Please."

The Forehand

Head up, turn perpendicular to the line of the ball, concentrate, watch the bounce, bring your arm back, keep your knees bent, be sure the racquet head is square to the ball, swing low to high for topspin and naturally follow through.

If you're remembering all these components of a good forehand shot, chances are the ball is now past you and can be found stuck in the chain link fence.

"If you snicker they leave quicker."

"Alright, let's pick them up and then
you can go home."

The Net

This is what it looks like when you play the net. Pretty big piece of territory you're trying to cover, isn't it, even if you could return the ball on your backhand side. What's more your opponent has the option of murdering or at least causing serious bodily harm to you with a ball to your exposed parts or lobbing a shot over your head which can cause a heart attack from running back for it.

The Net

When your opponent, however, reaches to the net it looks something like this. You can't really win with net play and I, for one, think it should be forbidden.

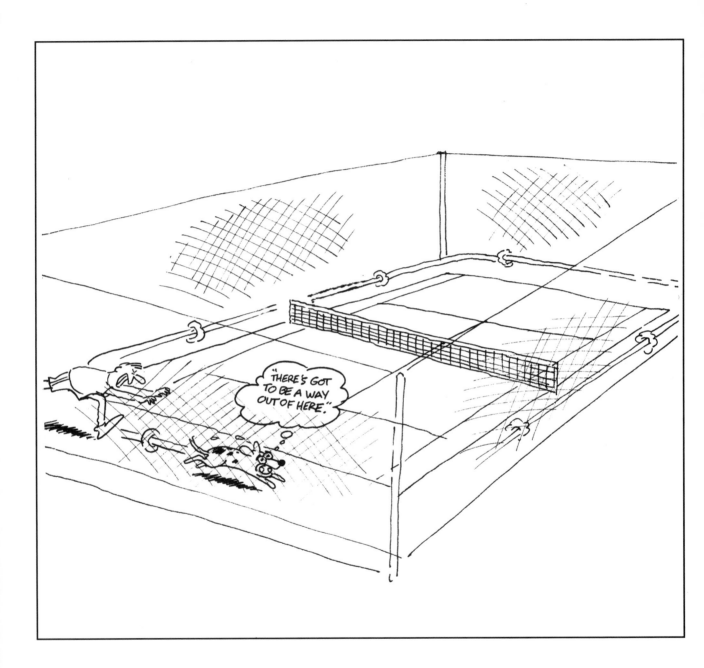

"Well, I say the season's over."

The Lob

It's hard enough to get the ball to land on the court, not to mention within the single lines, when you hit a regular stroke. Lobs can go anywhere, most often over fences where you'll have to crawl around in thorns and brambles to retrieve them. The safest approach to a lob is to hit a short wimpy one and hope the sun in your opponent's eye will win you the point.

The lob is a much more cunning shot on
an indoor court.

"It's all right, it's all right. I'm just getting him used to the idea."

"Chris is a fanatic about staying hydrated
on hot days."

Where Do Lost Balls Go?

First you should understand that in the history of tennis, no one has ever lost a dirty old dead ball. Fresh, clean, bouncy ones are the only balls that disappear. Tennis balls vanish in three ways.

---

1. On public courts, they're taken by players on adjoining courts who started off playing with dead dirty balls but go home with good ones. On club courts, they're stolen only if they land in or within three feet of a member's tennis bag.

Where Do Lost Balls Go?

2. They are hidden in underground holes by cute furry creatures who will bite you if you try to retrieve your property.

3. They are swallowed whole by poisonous tennis ball eating plants.

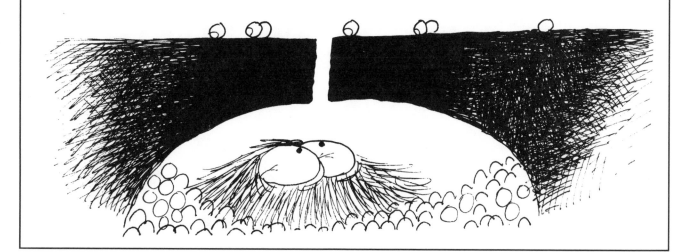

"Quit praying for a double fault, Father."

"Well, I say tie breakers are for sissies."

The Second Serve

OK, your rocket-like, bullet of a first serve is called out and you are faced with the dilemma of avoiding a double fault. You could try a medium powered serve but your cowardly mind cries out for a gentle nudge of the ball, safely over the net with an easy bent wrist pop, if only you can tolerate the snickers of the spectators.

"Whaddaya mean we're counting foot faults?"

"You're right, he is fast."

"Spence is such a sore loser."

What ants think about Tennis.

"But honey, the courts are lighted 'til 10."

Catching Your Breath

It's no fun being an aerobic cripple and gasping for breath after each point. The problem is cumulative and as you get more short of breath your opponent gets stronger and can run you back and forth more easily. The solution — you must employ one or more of the standard or advanced breath catching ploys.

Breath Catching Ploys

Standard	**Advanced**
1. Tying shoe lace	1. Removing shoe to get pebble and then checking under inner sole
2. Slowly picking up balls	2. Tapping balls to opponent but just out of reach, like over the fence
3. Arguing about score	3. Arguing about last set's score
4. Towel off forehead and handle	4. Check net height

"Matt was stretching before the game and
threw his back out."

"So this guy says, 'Try throwing it a little higher
when you serve.'"

The Psychological Game

The sophisticated player always carries more than one racquet to the court. Three or four will make even more of an impression. Bouncing the ball furiously before a serve and checking the net height are also good. I like to start right in serving with no warm up. I figure this way it'll take my opponent a few points before he realizes that I can't really serve at all.

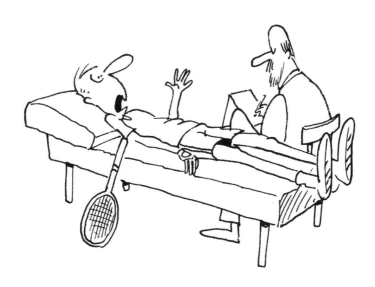

"Steve always brings three racquets to the court."

"Keep your eye on the ball, Mrs. Floresheim."

"I still think it's too high."

These other books are available at many fine stores.

#2350 Sailing. Using the head at night • Sex & Sailing • Monsters in the Ice Chest • How to look nautical in bars and much more nautical nonsense.

#2351 Computers. Where computers really are made • How to understand computer manuals without reading them • Sell your old $2,000,000 computer for $60 • Why computers are always lonely and much more solid state computer humor.

#2352 Cats. Living with cat hair • The advantages of kitty litter • Cats that fart • How to tell if you've got a fat cat.

#2353 Tennis. Where do lost balls go? • Winning the psychological game • Catching your breath • Perfecting wood shots.

#2354 Bowling. A book of bowling cartoons that covers: Score sheet cheaters • Boozers • Women who show off • Facing your team after a bad box and much more.

#2355 Parenting. Understanding the Tooth Fairy • 1000 ways to toilet train • Informers and tattle tales • Differences between little girls and little boys • And enough other information and laughs to make every parent wet their beds.

#2356 Fitness. T-shirts that will stop them from laughing at you • Earn big money with muscles • Sex and Fitness • Lose weight with laughter from this book.

#2357 Golf. Playing the psychological game • Going to the toilet in the rough • How to tell a real golfer • Some of the best golf cartoons ever printed.

#2358 Fishing. Handling 9" mosquitoes • Raising worms in your microwave oven • Neighborhood targets for fly casting practice • How to get on a first name basis with the Coast Guard plus even more.

#2359 Bathrooms. Why people love their bathroom • Great games to help pass the time on toilets • A frank discussion of bathroom odors • Plus lots of other stuff everyone out of diapers should know.

#2360 Biking. Why the wind is always against you • Why bike clothes are so tight • And lots of other stuff about what goes thunk, thunk, thunk when you pedal.

#2361 Running. How to "go" in the woods • Why running shoes cost more than sneakers • Keeping your lungs from bursting by letting the other guy talk.

Ivory Tower Publishing Co., Inc.   125 Walnut St., PO Box 9132, Watertown, MA 02272-9132
Telephone #: (617) 923-1111   Fax #: (617) 923-8839